Searchlight
BOOKS™

What's Cool
about Science?

Discover

Space
Exploration

Liz Kruesi

Lerner Publications ◆ Minneapolis

Content Consultant: Wallace T. Fowler, Professor, Aerospace Engineering and
Engineering Mechanics, The University of Texas at Austin

Lerner Publications Company
A division of Lerner Publishing Group, Inc.
241 First Avenue North
Minneapolis, MN 55401 USA

For reading levels and more information, look up this title at
www.lernerbooks.com.

Library of Congress Cataloging-in-Publication Data

Names: Kruesi, Liz, author.
Title: Discover space exploration / by Liz Kruesi.
Description: Minneapolis : Lerner Publications, [2017] | Series: Searchlight books. What's
    cool about science? | Audience: Ages 8–11. | Audience: Grades 4 to 6. | Includes
    bibliographical references and index.
Identifiers: LCCN 2015049915 (print) | LCCN 2016005680 (ebook) | ISBN 9781512408119
    (lb : alk. paper) | ISBN 9781512412901 (pb : alk. paper) | ISBN 9781512410693 (eb pdf)
Subjects: LCSH: Space sciences—Juvenile literature. | Manned space flight—Juvenile
    literature. | Outer space—Exploration—Juvenile literature. | Solar system—Juvenile
    literature.
Classification: LCC TL793 .K78 2017 (print) | LCC TL793 (ebook) | DDC 629.43/5—dc23

LC record available at http://lccn.loc.gov/2015049915

Manufactured in the United States of America
1 – VP – 7/15/16

Contents

Chapter 1

WHAT IS SPACE EXPLORATION?

People explore the universe in many ways. Astronauts fly into space. They have flown as far as Earth's moon. To explore more distant places, engineers and scientists launch machines. Robots have visited nearby planets and their moons. They send back pictures and information.

Astronauts explored the moon in the 1960s and 1970s. How do scientists explore more distant places?

To explore distant stars, scientists use powerful telescopes. Telescopes are devices that collect light. The light collected from distant stars can tell us a lot about the universe.

The Hubble Space Telescope circles Earth at a height of more than 340 miles (547 kilometers).

Our Neighborhood in Space

We live on the planet Earth. Our solar system has seven other planets. All the planets orbit the sun. Most of the planets have moons. The solar system contains other objects too. These are called asteroids, comets, and dwarf planets. They orbit the sun at great distances. Many of the solar system's planets, moons, asteroids, and dwarf planets have been visited by robotic spacecraft.

Earth is the only planet known to have life.

This galaxy is called NGC 4414. Each galaxy contains many stars.

But our solar system is only a small part of the universe. Most of the points of light in the night sky are stars. They are so far away that they look like points of light. But they are actually huge balls of gas like our sun. These stars are all within our own galaxy. Our galaxy is called the Milky Way Galaxy. It contains billions of stars. There are billions of other galaxies in the universe.

Telescopes on Earth and in space study these stars and galaxies. Some look for planets orbiting distant stars. Others look at what makes up galaxies. The newest telescopes study dark matter and dark energy. These things are invisible to the eye. Yet scientists have discovered they make up 95 percent of the mass of the universe.

MANY TELESCOPES ON EARTH ARE LOCATED ON TALL MOUNTAINS. THIS GIVES THEM A CLEARER VIEW OF SPACE.

Learning about dark matter and dark energy is one of the biggest mysteries in science today. Exploring space helps scientists make new discoveries about these and all the other secrets of the universe.

Each object in this image is a galaxy containing billions of stars. Many of these stars have planets of their own.

Chapter 2

HUMANS IN SPACE

The first human space traveler reached orbit in 1961. In 1969, two astronauts became the first people to walk on the moon. Since then, hundreds of other astronauts have flown into space.

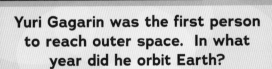

Yuri Gagarin was the first person to reach outer space. In what year did he orbit Earth?

Going into space requires special equipment. Astronauts ride inside a spacecraft. It protects them and holds supplies. Astronauts also wear special suits that provide air to breathe, keep them warm, and protect them from radiation.

To reach space, the spacecraft is placed atop a huge rocket. The rocket blasts off from Earth. It shoots high into the sky and gains amazing speed. Once the spacecraft reaches space, it circles the planet in orbit. Some spacecraft remain in orbit around Earth. Others use rocket engines to leave Earth's orbit and fly elsewhere in the solar system.

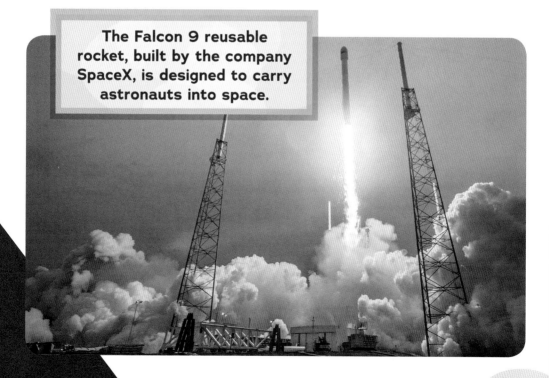

The Falcon 9 reusable rocket, built by the company SpaceX, is designed to carry astronauts into space.

Space Stations

Space stations are large spacecraft that orbit Earth. They are often made of many connected sections. Some sections have science labs. Others have places for astronauts to sleep. Huge solar panels outside turn sunlight into electricity. This keeps equipment running. People live and carry out experiments inside space stations.

One early space station was called Skylab. It was launched in 1973.

THE INTERNATIONAL SPACE STATION CIRCLES EARTH ABOUT EVERY NINETY MINUTES.

▼

The largest space station is the International Space Station (ISS). Many countries around the world worked together to build it. More than two hundred astronauts from different nations have spent time on the ISS since the year 2000.

In 2015, US astronaut Scott Kelly flew to the ISS. He prepared to live there for a full year. His twin brother, Mark, stayed on Earth. During the year, scientists ran medical tests on the brothers. The research helped them learn how being in space affects human beings.

Scott Kelly (*right*) and his brother Mark (*left*) were interviewed before Scott's mission began.

Mars has been nicknamed "the Red Planet" for its reddish color.

Going to Mars

People have never been farther from Earth than the moon. But scientists want to send people to more distant places. They plan to send humans to the planet Mars in the 2030s.

Mars is very far away. It may take up to nine months to get there. Engineers will need to design a powerful rocket to launch the astronauts. They will also need to make a spacecraft that can keep the astronauts safe for a long time. With these tools, humans will be able to explore Mars and other places in the solar system.

Space Lettuce

A trip to Mars and back to Earth will take a few years. Astronauts will need a lot of food in that time. Rather than packing food, scientists want to grow food in space. A project on the ISS has succeeded in growing lettuce. In 2015, astronauts tasted it for the first time. Next they will try to grow other vegetables. Two options are cabbage and peppers.

The lettuce eaten on the ISS took thirty-three days to grow.

Chapter 3

EXPLORING THE SOLAR SYSTEM

Humans have not yet traveled to another planet. But we have sent spacecraft to other worlds. These machines carry tools that help scientists learn about distant places. Cameras send back clear images. Sensors examine what materials make up planets and moons. Computers help these tools work together to explore the universe.

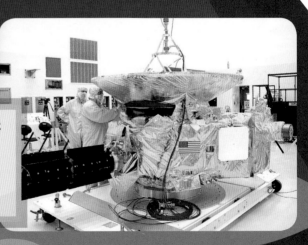

Scientists and engineers test spacecraft before sending them out into the solar system. What kinds of tools do spacecraft carry?

Some robot explorers land on a planet and move around. Others circle a planet or moon in space, studying it for years at a time. Or they may only fly by an object once, taking pictures as they zoom past it. Each type of mission has an important role in space exploration.

The Mars Reconnaissance Orbiter takes highly detailed images, such as this one, from less than 200 miles (322 km) above the Martian surface.

The Curiosity rover is about the size of a small car.

Red Rovers

Other than Earth, Mars is one of the most-explored places in the solar system. Today robots drive along the surface. They are known as rovers. They scoop, drill, and study soil. The latest rover is named Curiosity. It arrived in 2012. Other robotic spacecraft take pictures from orbit around Mars.

One major goal of exploring Mars is to find water. Life on Earth needs water to survive. If water can be found on Mars, it may mean life is there too. The robots that study Mars have seen features that look like dry riverbeds and seas. In 2015, one orbiting spacecraft spotted liquid water dripping down a slope on the surface. The exciting discovery encouraged scientists to keep studying Mars.

SCIENTISTS BELIEVE THE DARK LINES IN THIS 2015 PHOTO OF MARS SHOW WHERE WATER HAS FLOWED DOWN A HILL.

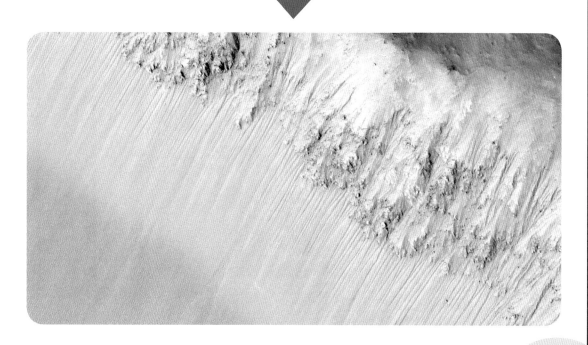

Orbiting Giant Planets

Jupiter and Saturn are giant planets made of gas. Jupiter is the solar system's largest planet. Saturn is known for its beautiful rings. Both planets have interesting moons.

Jupiter has an enormous storm known as the Great Red Spot.

This artist's image shows Cassini entering orbit around Saturn.

The Cassini spacecraft has been orbiting Saturn since 2004. It has photographed lakes and rivers on Saturn's biggest moon, Titan. It also found rain and clouds. But these things are not made of water. Instead, they are liquid methane, possibly mixed with some water ice.

Cassini also found water on a different moon of Saturn. The moon is called Enceladus. It has huge geysers. They spurt water from an underground ocean.

Jupiter's moon Europa has an ocean of water. A shell of cracked ice floats above it. The Galileo spacecraft made these discoveries about Europa. Scientists have plans to send more robots to further explore Europa.

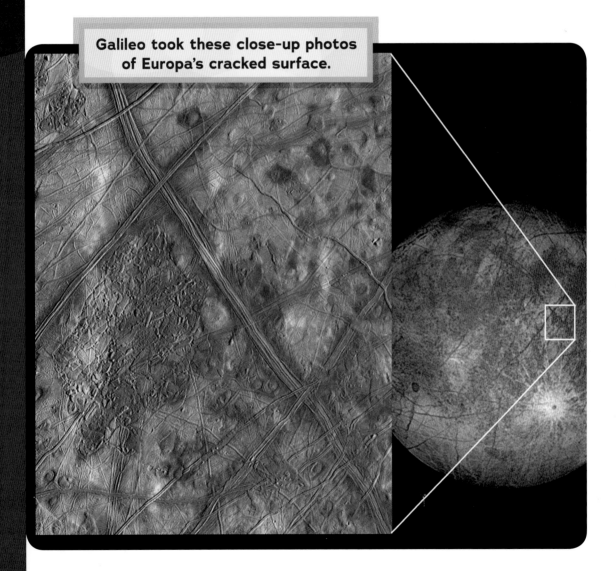

Galileo took these close-up photos of Europa's cracked surface.

To Europa

In 2015, NASA started work on a robotic spacecraft that will visit Europa. It will launch in the 2020s. The spacecraft will fly past the moon forty-five times. It will have cameras and other tools. One tool will measure how thick the moon's ice shell is. It will look for thinner ice and pockets of warm water. Similar places on Earth's continent Antarctica have life. Scientists want to know whether life might exist on Europa too.

This artist's image shows NASA's planned Europa spacecraft and the path of its orbit.

This photo was taken by Mariner 4, the first spacecraft to fly past Mars. It reached Mars in 1965.

Flybys

To enter orbit, spacecraft must slow down as they approach the planet. They fire their rocket engines to slow down. But some spacecraft are too small to do this. They have no room for rockets or the fuel that powers the rockets. Instead of entering orbit, these spacecraft fly past the object they are studying. They take pictures and collect data as they fly by.

New Horizons took this photo
on July 14, 2015, when it was
closest to Pluto.

New Horizons was an important flyby spacecraft. It
launched from Earth in 2006. It reached the dwarf
planet Pluto in 2015. The spacecraft spent just a few
days studying Pluto at close range. New Horizons took
the clearest pictures of the dwarf planet yet. It revealed
icy mountains and broad plains on Pluto's surface.

Chapter 4

SPACE TELESCOPES

The universe is huge. Spacecraft cannot reach other stars within human lifetimes. Instead we use telescopes to study these distant objects. Telescopes and their cameras collect the light that stars and galaxies give off.

Space telescopes look deep into the sky to study the most distant known galaxies. Why do scientists use telescopes to study space?

Human eyes see only one kind of light. But telescopes collect many types of light. Earth's atmosphere blocks some of these types of light, including X-rays. So scientists send telescopes into space to study them.

The Hubble Space Telescope was launched into space aboard the space shuttle *Discovery*.

EARTH'S ATMOSPHERE CAN MAKE IT DIFFICULT FOR TELESCOPE USERS ON THE GROUND TO CLEARLY SEE OBJECTS IN SPACE.

Earth's atmosphere also blurs the light from space objects. This is what makes stars appear to twinkle. Space telescopes orbit outside the atmosphere. This lets scientists see stars and galaxies clearly.

Other Planets

One goal of today's space telescopes is to find distant planets. To do this, scientists aim the telescopes at faraway stars. Sometimes a star gets dimmer, then goes back to its original brightness. This means that a planet is orbiting the star. The planet briefly passed between the star and the telescope. It blocked some of the star's light.

Orbiting planets only block a tiny bit of a star's light.

The Kepler telescope has been in space since 2009. It watches for these dips in brightness. It has found more than one thousand planets this way.

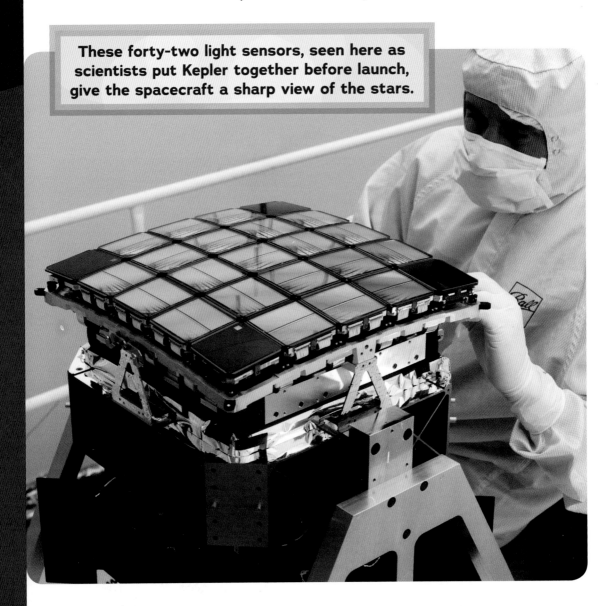

These forty-two light sensors, seen here as scientists put Kepler together before launch, give the spacecraft a sharp view of the stars.

Space Starshade

Looking directly at distant planets can be hard. Glare from their stars can hide these planets from view. Scientists have a new idea that can help. They plan to put a huge, flower-shaped shade into space. It will fly thousands of miles in front of a space telescope. The shade will block the light from a star. It will make it easier to see that star's planets.

This artist's image shows the planned starshade as it separates from its telescope.

Dark Universe

Everything in the universe has mass. Mass is a measure of how much material is in an object. The amount of mass an object has affects how the object moves in space. A force called gravity pulls objects with mass together.

This photo was taken from the moon. Gravity is the force that formed the moons and planets and now holds the moon in Earth's orbit.

THE LIGHT FROM DISTANT GALAXIES CAN BE BENT BY STRONG GRAVITY.

Scientists can measure the mass of objects they can see. They can also measure gravity. These measurements led to a major mystery. The gravity in the universe appears to be too strong. Visible objects do not have enough mass to cause this gravity. Scientists have been searching for a solution to this problem.

Scientists have detected likely dark matter in this group of galaxies. In this image, they have highlighted a ring of it in blue.

Many scientists believe invisible materials are causing the gravity. These things are known as dark matter. Another mysterious force is causing the universe to expand faster than expected. It is known as dark energy. Scientists do not know what dark matter and dark energy are. But they have found many clues that these mysterious things exist.

New telescopes will launch in the 2020s. They will help us learn more about dark matter and dark energy. They will search for answers about our mysterious universe.

The James Webb Space Telescope is scheduled to launch in 2018. Its light-collecting mirrors are seven times larger than the mirror of the Hubble Space Telescope.

Glossary

astronaut: a human who travels in space

dark energy: a mysterious energy that makes the universe expand

dark matter: an invisible material that causes gravitational forces in space

gravity: a force that pulls things together. Gravity keeps people on Earth's surface and holds stars, gas, and dust together in a galaxy.

Milky Way Galaxy: our home galaxy

robot: a machine that can move and makes decisions on its own

solar system: our home neighborhood in space. It holds our sun, eight planets, dozens of moons, and countless smaller asteroids and comets made of rock and ice.

star: a ball of glowing, hot gas

telescope: a tool made of lenses or mirrors that collects light from a distant object, like a star or a planet

Learn More about Space Exploration

Books

Kops, Deborah. *Exploring Space Robots*. Minneapolis, MN: Lerner Publications, 2012. Learn more about the robotic spacecraft that explore our solar system's planets and moons.

Richards, Jon, and Ed Simkins. *Record-Breaking Earth & Space Facts*. Minneapolis, MN: Lerner Publications, 2015. Find out which planet has the largest moon, the biggest mountain, and many other records.

Stott, Carole. *Space Exploration*. New York: DK Children, 2014. Explore the solar system and space technology.

Websites

Eyes on Exoplanets
http://eyes.nasa.gov/eyes-on-exoplanets.html
Explore the planets that scientists have found around other stars.

HubbleSite
http://hubblesite.org
The Hubble Space Telescope has made many discoveries about the universe and has taken thousands of beautiful photos. Learn about the discoveries and explore these photos at this website.

The Space Place
http://spaceplace.nasa.gov
Check out space-related facts, puzzles, games, and activities.

Index

Photo Acknowledgments

The images in this book are used with the permission of: NASA, pp. 4, 5, 6, 7, 9, 12, 13, 14, 15, 16, 17, 18, 19, 20, 21, 22, 23, 24, 25, 26, 27, 28, 29, 32, 33, 34, 35, 36, 37; © voshadhi/iStock.com, p. 8; © AP Images, p. 10; SpaceX, p. 11; © inhauscreative/iStock.com, p. 30; © Mark Garlick/Science Source, p. 31.

Front Cover: NASA.

Main body text set in Adrianna Regular 14/20.
Typeface provided by Chank.